Succulents

for

the Garden

Attila Kapitany and Rudolf Schulz

Second edition, copyright 2006. Attila Kapitany and Rudolf Schulz

ISBN 0 958516723

Schulz Publishing
Box 40, Teesdale, VIC 3328, Australia
www.tarrex.com
tarrex@ozemail.com.au
gecko@connexus.net.au

Printed by Everbest Printing Co Ltd, China

Acknowledgements

We thank:
Ruth Bancroft, Clive Blazey, Fiona Brockhoff, Bert and Mia Coppus, Marie D'Alton, Pat Dixon, Brian Gerrard, Jim and Julie Hall, Michele Kapitany, Judy Leadbetter, William Martin, Diana Morgan, Roni Nettleton, Matthew Snowdon, Bev Spiller and Walter Teague.

We also thank all the passionate succulent gardeners who have helped inspire us for this book and have allowed us to photograph their plants or gardens.

Contents

Introduction

WANTED! A grow anywhere low care plant which is easily established and needs no special maintenance or regular training, staking or pruning. The plant should not be invasive or grow too large or become too untidy and must be reasonably priced. If this is what you are after, then succulents are the answer to your needs.

In gardening terms succulents are a group of plants that store water in their swollen leaves, stems and/or roots. The spiny succulents as a whole generally belong to the cactus family, which this book only briefly

An old fashioned rural fence has been recently underplanted with *Echeveria* 'Imbricata' to maintain the look of the past. Ironically, to many this is now the look of the future.

The impressive selection on the market today makes designing a garden using succulents very challenging.

covers. Instead, we will lead you through the fascinating world of the 'other succulents', those wonderful fat leafed plants so ideally suited to outdoor containers and general garden uses. There are many thousands of succulents available and this book in no way attempts to cover them all. Instead, we present only those which have a proven record of performing well in many parts of Australia. In particular, we present some succulents that have been either neglected by other books or are new to nurseries.

Most succulents prefer sunny conditions, which create compact growth and bring out their brilliant colours, and are able to take all the sun that is available. Succulents growing outdoors have much more intensely coloured foliage, grow more vigorously and often produce more prolific blooms than indoor specimens. The most dramatic outdoor effects are usually obtained in situations with afternoon sun and poor soil.

With the advent of water-wise gardening there has been an increased awareness of how much water is consumed by plants and the trend today is to minimise this use. The urban land authorities in conjunction with state water boards are now in the forefront of implementing new low water technologies. Water-efficient demonstration gardens and advisory boards already exist in Darwin, Hobart, Canberra and Melbourne. The information they provide explains how to create water-efficient gardens for your area. This may include lists of plants especially suited to your area which can be planted with the succulents covered in this book to create a garden which, once established, will look good and also save you money.

Compared to traditional garden plants, succulents require lower levels of maintenance, especially time spent on watering, weeding and pruning. In our era of resource conservation, self-maintenance is a highly desirable trait for all ornamental plants. Succulents are also ideal candidates for use in today's water-wise garden, not only because of their versatility but because of the tremendous variety of shapes, forms, textures, colours and flowers which they exhibit. But above all, the ideal low water use plant is cope with considerable neglect while still looking good.

Where and how to display succulents is limited only by your imagination. Here bricks, terracotta pipes, pots and a birdbath have transformed an exposed, windy west facing site with no access to taps. The shallow raised beds are on a compacted gravel or concrete surface.

One of the many low growing mesemb groundcovers.

In this book we will show you how to successfully use succulents in many of your garden's problem areas. Consider the following:

1.   When soils are too poor for annuals, think succulents.
2.   When the slope is so steep that every plant fails, think succulents.
3.   When temperatures fluctuate to threatening extremes, think succulents.
4.   When rain fails to come and nothing seems to survive, think succulents.
5.   When you are tired of watering and paying high water bills, think succulents.

Why and where succulents are a better choice than natives in a water-wise garden.

1.   Succulents do not have deep roots and are not invasive. Plants with deep or invasive roots such as eucalypts and acacias can drain every last bit of water out of the soil, which can lead to nearby plants being starved of water even if regularly watered.

2.   Natives, because of their great water extraction ability, can often upset the water balance in the soil in a way that affects house foundations, leading to cracking in walls. Succulents, because they are shallow rooted, will never cause cracking.
3.   Many natives are messy and when faced with drought, shed leaves and even branches to stay alive. Succulents shrink in size as they lose water but seldom shed large numbers of leaves.

Small growing mesembs such as *Mossia intervallaris* and *Faucaria tigrina* (right) always remain neat and tidy.

4.   Well grown succulents remain neat and trim and do not develop that leggy, scraggly look that many natives do after only a few years.
5.   Most native plants do not tolerate heavy pruning as is sometimes required for painting, plumbing work or the erection of a new fence. Succulents can be heavily pruned and easily transplanted without risk of death or undue stress.

6. Natives burn readily, while most succulents do not. If your home is in a bush-fire prone area, this alone could save your house and possibly people's lives.

Close-up of *Echeveria* 'Black Prince'. After flowering, it may be worthwhile removing dried or dead flower stems.

Where succulents shine

Coastal areas. Because many succulents are salt tolerant, they can tolerate the salty winds and soil common to coastal gardens.

In windy areas. The compact growth and stiff stems of most succulents make them ideal for exposed hilltops and other windy sites.

Under trees. Trees compete tremendously for water and their invasive roots often make gardening difficult using conventional plants. Many succulents, because they have shallow roots and can stand long periods without rain, grow quite happily in this difficult gardening situation.

As ground covers. Many growing ground covers can become invasive and require weeding, spraying and constant vigilance as well as watering. Succulents, while slower to become established, are well suited as ground covers in a variety of situations.

Where bushfires are a risk. All non-succulent plants pose a fire hazard, no matter how green or low growing. Most succulents will not burn and may be considered the best living fire retardant available.

In shallow soils. Hillside homes are becoming more popular but unfortunately they often have little soil depth in the garden. Rather than spend a fortune on buying in soil, which often contains weeds or lots of organic material which will quickly disappear, why not plant succulents on these difficult sites?

Narrow garden areas. Strips along driveways and fences are often difficult to maintain and water. Shrubs often need staking and become leggy. Such areas make ideal succulent gardens which will require little or no watering once established.

Around the pool. Tired of dealing with leaves in the pool from all those messy shrubs? As an alternative, think succulents!

Borders. Tired of that tatty and boring English box border which requires trimming all too regularly? Many succulents offer an alternative and will provide much more interest and colour in your borders.

Steep slopes. Where the water just runs off. Forget watering! Plant the right succulents and that slope will be covered and maintained with a minimum of fuss.

With bulbs. Many spring bulbs such as daffodils need to have their unsightly foliage retained until well into summer, leaving the area looking untidy. Why not plant succulents among your bulbs? Unlike conventional ground covers which can be deep rooted and compete with bulbs for nutrients, succulents are shallow rooted and not gross feeders. Unlike most ground covers, succulents do not need to be watered just at the time when the bulbs need to dry off.

New homes. New brick houses often have a lot of mortar rubble just under the shallow layer of topsoil which is usually added to a new home's garden. Most conventional garden plants object to high concentrations of lime, as well as the compaction that building a new home brings to the garden area. Most succulents, on the other hand, tolerate lime rich soils and do not object to compaction and shallow soil.

Senecio mandraliscae is used here with tulips. The shallow root system of succulents and their tolerance of drought makes them ideal as companions with winter growing bulbs.

Aeoniums are hardy shrubs and make good borders.

Succulents – a variety of colours, shapes and textures.
(left) *Trichodiadema bulbosum*
(above) *Sedum nussbaumerianum*
(below) One of the many *Puya* species.

The use of succulents in cemeteries has a long history. Succulents are perfect as grave adornments as shown in this series of photographs. This *Echeveria pulvinata* has survived for over a year on only natural rainfall and may outlive its cracking plastic pot. Compared to the lifeless bunch of fading plastic flowers, this flower-like echeveria symbolises everlasting life in a colourful and stylish way. Perhaps it was a favourite plant of the deceased?
(below) Intense sunlight and low nutrient levels cause a colourful reddish tinge on many succulents.

Chapter 1
Location and succulent growth

Most of Australia has a dry and sunny climate which is very different from the damp temperate climates of England and northern Europe. The heavily populated coastal fringe of the Australian southern states have climatic conditions similar to California and the Mediterranean coast where cool wet winters and drier summers are the norm. In these areas a great variety of succulents will perform at their best, providing an almost unlimited choice of growth forms, colours and texture suitable for most garden situations.

Not all of the succulents described in this book will perform at their best in all areas; rather, they have diverse preferences with some growing better than others in a particular location. Some succulents will grow well in every part of Australia.

Elevation plays an important part in determining how succulents will perform. In subtropical areas such as Sydney, some winter growing succulents find the high humidity and rain in summer difficult. In the elevated areas such as Bowral, succulents do better, mainly because the humidity is lower. The succulents which grow well in the subtropical regions of the north NSW coast are often different from those discussed in this book, however many will be quite suitable.

This aloe hedge looks spiky and keeps traffic at a distance but is actually soft to touch (see flowers on page 52).

Light frosts (0 to -3°C) seldom pose a problem for most succulents in the garden and usually result in no more than some leaf tip 'burn' on the tender species. Moderate frosts (-4 to -6°C) pose additional risks, with heavy frosts (-7°C or lower) often limiting the choice of succulents to those which are truly hardy (of which there are many species). Areas which receive heavy frosts can create special problems for succulents: because succulents contain large amounts of water in their leaves, some are damaged by freezing. Some, like the popular *Agave attenuata*, tolerate only light frosts. This species however, grows exceptionally well in the subtropics and tropics where it is occasionally seen mixed with bananas and tropical foliage. Several succulents grow well in tropical regions including all kalanchoes, some echeverias and several of the Mexican sedums. So how will you know which succulents will thrive in your area? With other plants it is often just a matter of walking the streets and looking into neighbouring gardens to see what grows well. While this works for some of the more common succulents, many of the species described in this book were until recently uncommon in cultivation and will often not be found in established gardens. This means that some trial and error will be necessary for some of the species that we describe. For areas with moderate to heavy frosts, a year's growth under the protection of foliage is recommended for those species

In this arrangement of succulents something is in flower all the time. As soon as one finishes flowering, another starts. Planting in groupings of the same plants, all of the same age and size creates consistency in appearance which is desirable in today's gardens.

A long dead lawn with an abandoned flower bed. And what has survived and is looking good without any maintenance whatsoever? *Crassula ovata.*

which are not specifically mentioned as being tolerant of heavy frosts.

Gardeners in areas away from the coast will need to consider the problems caused by excessive summer heat. Unlike most cactus, which tolerate high heat levels well, some succulents are rather tender and will actually cook if in full sun the whole day in above 40°C temperatures, especially if this comes after a period of cool or cloudy weather which seems to act like a sudden shock to the system. While only the most exposed leaves will be damaged, it can mean that these plants require some protection from the afternoon sun. A visit to some of the established cactus and succulent gardens such as those listed on page 95 will better prepare inland gardeners for what will survive and what will not. Gardeners on the coast who are not familiar with succulents may wish to visit nurseries which have succulent display gardens such as Collector's Corner at Garden World in Melbourne, which is in a frost-free area.

Some facts about succulents

Contrary to most people's beliefs, succulents are not desert plants. Most grow in semi-arid or temperate areas which receive regular rain each year. Often they grow in areas with either poor soils, shallow soils or rocky places where soil is at a minimum. Succulents do not compete well with dense tree and shrub growth as they need more sunlight than is received when growing in a forest. Succulents are also not totally resistant to fires, especially if growing among highly flammable tall grasses or shrubs. In nature most succulents grow in places where other plants find it too difficult and it is just this feature that makes them so adaptable for a garden situation.

Succulents usually have a shallow root system which allows them to utilise the water from small amounts of rainfall. In completely dry soil, the root hairs of almost all plants die off and will only regrow once the soil is moist again. Succulents have an amazing ability to regrow their root hairs and many are able to absorb water within twenty-four hours after rain. As a result, their leaves, which have the ability to swell to many times their desiccated weight, gain water, which is

stored until needed. This allows succulents to grow even when the soil is dry. The shallow roots of succulents are not invasive.

The shallow root system is one of the great garden attributes of succulents as it makes them less competitive with other garden plants, allowing them to be interplanted without fear of 'stealing' water or affecting deeper rooted plants. The quick root regrowth ability of succulents, coupled with their shallow roots, allows them to be transplanted easily. Often they can be simply lifted up by their stems and placing them on the surface of the soil in their new location. A spade is usually not required. What could be easier than that?

(above) Large trees often expose their roots. Watering shallow soil before planting gives the best results as very few plants can survive such dry conditions.
(below) Careful choice of plants or some experimentation can be very helpful. Here *Echeveria elegans* has managed not only to survive, but to thrive in deep shade and in very moist conditions amongst "babies tears".

Succulents can actually tolerate a lot more water than most gardeners imagine. A wide selection of succulents grow quite well in tropical gardens where monsoonal rains can bring heavy downpours almost every day. As long as the soil is raised up to give good drainage, they thrive. This ability to tolerate wet soils during their growing season makes them more suitable as ground covers than conventional plants in the garden. Why not interplant succulents between and under your newly planted shrubs to fill in that empty space? With many shrubs, such as roses, camellias and any species which is trained as a standard, the stems are bare of foliage and unsightly. Succulents are ideal fill-ins in such situations. Once the shrubs fill out, the succulents can be easily replanted elsewhere. They will provide little competition for either nutrients or water and do not need to be watered at all. This is especially useful for gardeners who use drippers for watering as these need only be laid to the shrubs. An added advantage of this will be that the space in between the watered plants will remain drier, thus reducing weed growth.

High light levels are appreciated by almost all succulents. The higher the light level the more compact the growth and the better the leaf colouration. Sunny locations will produce healthier and more colourful plants than shady spots.

While succulents are hardy, health considerations are still important. If you suspect disease and pest infestation, throw out or destroy the old and sickly plants and buy or propagate new ones. It is possible to propagate 'replacements' for many species

Livingstone daisies. *Dorotheanthus bellidoniformis* is a winter/spring annual that can cheer up a bare garden very quickly.

of succulents by taking healthy cuttings, which once established, can be used to replace old and diseased plants. In the case of insects, succulents often have soil borne pests in the form of root mealy bugs, vine weevils or nematodes. All of these can be difficult to eradicate safely and easily. By using or growing replacement plants it is possible to keep disease and pests at bay without using dangerous time-consuming chemical remedies.

(above) *Sedum rubrotinctum* used as a bedding plant.
(left) Some of the echeverias which are now available from nurseries.
(below) *Aloe plicatilis* growing with *Euphorbia flanaganii* and *Echeveria* 'Imbricata'.

(above) Echeverias mix well with other garden plants and their bright foliage contrasts well with conifers.
(right) *Senecio mandriliscae* with *Strelitzia reginae*.
(below) Succulents provide year-round interest when planted in large bowls. The symmetrical shape of many succulents makes them ideal for geometric plantings.

Chapter 2

Water-wise gardening

Water-wise gardening is based on the princi-
ple that plants with similar requirements
should be grown together. At its most basic,
water-wise gardening theory divides the garden into three zones, in which plants with
similar water requirements are grown together.
Today, with soaring water charges and with
water conservation in mind, gardeners and
home owners are coming to terms with this
fundamental concept.

(right) Succulents are ideal for a dry and windy corner,
especially under eaves. In this picture, echeverias and
Nolina recurvata are being grown.
(below) These street-facing succulents are well away
from a hose or sprinkler and only require occasional
watering.

The inner zone of water-wise gardens usually incorporates plants with high water demands. In this tasteful selection, succulents are mixed with tender annuals.

The inner and most intensively planted garden area (high water zone) is usually near the house or where traffic is greatest and where water is most available. This is where gardeners should grow plants requiring frequent watering during dry weather such as annuals, vegetables, large leafed perennials and flower pots. The high water zone might be different for every house on the street. Even if the houses are identical, each garden will differ in layout, composition and style. One owner might wish to keep the front garden watered and have a lawn with annual borders. Another might prefer a vegetable garden behind the house and a herb garden near the back door while allowing the front garden to be in a lower water zone. With larger houses, the barbecue and pool areas might be in the high water zone. Some gardeners consider the back door to be their primary entry to the residence and practical people might keep their potted plants here for easy watering. Another family might want the front door and its environment to have a lush tropical look and plant it heavily with water-loving plants. The high water zone might be watered only with a hose or it might be under drip irrigation with a computerised watering system based on moisture sensors. The level of watering required is the key similarity, not the method of applying water.

The mowing and keeping of large open lawns can be very wasteful of time, space and, more importantly, of water in summer. Note the dead patches of lawn in the foreground. Behind the mower is *Agave attenuata*. It averages no more than 10 minutes attention a year, if that.

The middle zone in water-wise gardening is where plants do not receive watering for most of the year except during dry spells when water would be applied to correct major moisture deficits. Perennials, shrubs, fruit trees, some tender natives and other woody plants are grown in this zone. Often, much of the front garden falls within this category and this is the zone most often neglected since the amount of time needed to water it is often more than the time available. Succulents and other hardy plants can reduce this area, thus freeing up time which would have been spent on summer watering.

The outer zone in a water-wise garden might not be watered at all except during extreme dry spells. Typical areas would be along the driveway and along fences, at the edges of the property, the nature strip, and any area where the hose does not easily reach. Plants ideally suited to this area are

This area next to a residence is not in a high traffic area and does not get the maintenance it requires to keep it weed free. Birds flicked out any mulch and weeds and soil kept spilling through the rock cracks creating a constant problem until the introduction of a gap filler using *Echeveria secunda*. The added colour and contrast of shapes has also created a more interesting garden.

most of the larger growing natives and, of course, succulents. Many gardeners have found to their distress that native trees can become a problem, being messy, a fire hazard and hard on gutters and drains as well as quickly growing too large for the garden. A bill of $2000 is not uncommon for the removal of a single mature eucalyptus which might have cost $5 when it was planted fifteen or twenty years ago. Today, most gardeners realise that the plants in the garden must be kept in scale with its area. Large trees and shrubs are losing favour, to be replaced by a host of water-wise plants, with succulents being ideally suited.

Gardens designed around the water-wise theme will use at least 50% less water than conventional gardens and sometimes 80% less. This translates into a significant cost saving now that water charges are fully based on usage. The other obvious benefit is that the gardener needs to spend less time watering. A less obvious, but perhaps more important, benefit is that the plants grow better in a water-wise garden because they are growing together with other species requiring similar amounts of water. An example of a less water-wise garden would be roses planted together with native shrubs. It is likely that more water will be given to the roses than if they were growing on their own since the native shrubs will be taking more than their share. As most gardeners know, watering roses frequently, especially with a hose, increases the risk of black spot so that the rose and native garden would have less healthy roses

This large brick wall was erected to protect the house by blocking the westerly sun and wind. To the right is the dusty driveway which had been bare for over 20 years. Note: This photo was taken one year after planting with succulents.

This strip garden is well away from the house and has been planted with *Echeveria* 'Imbricata'.

A water-wise garden need not look dry and bare. With clever design it can look as rich, full and colourful as any garden. Note how full and yet diverse the plants in this picture are.

and some of the natives might develop root rot from all the unnecessary water.

The ideas presented in the water-wise garden theory are self-evident to many who have observed, grown and maintained plants for any length of time. Some experienced gardeners reading this will no doubt be patting themselves on the back for having done this for many years, well before the term 'water-wise' was coined.

Garden design

Garden design brings results. Gardens are judged by the condition and layout of their plants and by their presentation. While gardens can develop haphazardly and often do, they are usually less pleasing to the eye and contain inherent faults which will cause problems in future years. Poor planning, or worse still, none at all, may result in trees

dominating the garden which will cost large sums of money to remove when they become a hazard. Clogged drains, poor runoff and flooding can all be avoided with a well thought out garden design. Poor drainage is one of the most obvious signs that a garden has not been well designed in the first place.

The easiest way to achieve a complete garden 'make over' or to set up a new garden is to go to a professional design service with your general ideas and a list of your preferred plants and let them come up with different options for a new garden. Make it clear that you want a water-wise garden and that succulents are part of your plan. Ask to see their work and consider their fees, keeping in mind that a well designed and executed garden will add substantially to the value of your property as well as give you pleasure for years to come. The time to renovate your garden is *now*, not when you are about to sell your house. Those with a limited budget may choose to use a professional designer only for the design service and do the actual garden work themselves. Even if this is done in stages taking months or even years to complete, an investment in design will ensure that fundamental design principles and sound layout have been applied.

Home owners do not need to start from scratch when considering a designed garden as many of the existing garden elements can be retained in the new plan. Often only a small portion of a garden is in need of rejuvenation. Instead of just ripping out a shrub or two and shoving some other plants into the gap, why not design a garden plan and develop the whole area? Existing succulents can be easily removed from other sections of your garden and incorporated into your plan. With the addition of some new and exciting species, a whole new look can be given to that tired and run-down looking part of your garden. Another possibility for a small new garden section is to reduce the area of lawn. Or perhaps your nature strip is in need of some radical reworking. Even a large container can be a study in garden design. Size is no object in achieving a pleasing and well organised design, as long as some basic principles are applied.

Some points to consider: a garden is very much a part of your home and some of it will be in constant view. Consider where you will view your garden from the most and try to picture a pleasing scene. Different windows should present varied scenes. A well planned garden can be a beautiful all year round feast for the eyes.

Consider the non-living components in your garden design: paving, a terrace, a small pool. All need to be considered and planned for. Visit your garden centre and examine the new materials and garden aids which are now available for outdoor use. Furniture, edging, containers, watering systems and plants have come a long way since the days of basic natives, red geraniums and railway sleepers.

This looks anything but desert like. A reddish *Phormium* is interplanted with *Senecio mandraliscae* as an understorey.

(above) Annual succulents (*Portulaca grandiflora*) help brighten and fill this small newly planted garden bed. (right) With time, these fast ground-covering sedums may be crowded out by the larger echeverias. In the meantime they act as fillers as well as weed suppressers. (below) A semi-shaded garden under large trees has been brightened up, as has an old disused bird bath that was previously full of old leaves and mosquito larvae.

Chapter 3
Solving problems with succulents

While looking good in pots, most succulents generally perform better when planted in the garden. This is because the roots are unrestricted and have access to more nutrients and water. As a result, plants grow more vigorously, producing flowers on a regular basis. In sunny locations, growth will be compact and colours will be bright.

With good drainage, many succulents will tolerate more water outdoors in summer than many gardeners realise, allowing them to be used in high water areas, especially

A cleverly constructed 'living ball' of *Echeveria secunda*

Sedum dasyphyllum is a low, mat forming ground cover which will tolerate some shade. Here, a large and small growing variety grow together.

those watered by drippers or micro-sprinklers. Succulents thrive in areas not covered by watering systems and will be able to compete with most weed growth. Remember that weeds grow well only when watered, and by reducing the moisture in the soil weed growth will slow, giving slower growing succulents an even chance of keeping up in the competition for light, space, water and food.

Ground covers

Low maintenance ground covers are now being used to reduce the size of the lawn area and are becoming a popular alternative to lawns themselves. Lawns rarely grow well under trees and are difficult to maintain on uneven or steep slopes. Succulents are not normally thought of as suitable for ground covers. In fact, they are ideally suited to low-traffic areas if certain criteria are met.

Temporary ground covers

New gardens are often very bare and open areas without any trees or shade. Often the most common starting point is the introduction of a few seedling trees or large shrubs which will eventually become specimen plants giving future shade. What can be used to fill in the spaces between these plants until they grow sufficiently large to fill the space with their foliage? Succulents are the ideal ground cover, being shallow rooted. Since the feature plants are still small, they do not require the heavy watering of mature plants, and this suits succulents. Many traditional ground covers will compete with the feature plants or become invasive and have to be laboriously removed once the feature plants fill out their allotted spaces. On the other hand, shallow rooted succulents can be easily removed and replanted elsewhere, saving money and work at the same time. Succulents do not suffer stress unduly from being uprooted and will often benefit greatly from being divided and moved after a number of years. This feature allows succulents to be viewed as relocatable ground covers which increase in value as each season progresses. As an added bonus, succulents also surpress weeds.

Ground covers where large tree roots are common and exposed

Mature trees often produce such a thick surface layer of roots that most neighbouring plants are suppressed even when adequate

This mixture of aeoniums, aloes, cotyledons and senecios is growing under a native tree where few other plants would thrive.

water and sunlight is available. Cypresses are especially troublesome as their root system can extend away from the trunk up to twice the tree height. Succulents survive and can thrive in this environment but will need supplementary watering until well established (usually for one complete growing season). Planting succulents near invasive trees can actually be an advantage as the trees will often keep the soil from becoming too soggy, even during the winter, when many of the hardy succulents are in growth. In southern areas such as Victoria, mature trees growing on the western sides of gardens will intercept much of the rain with their foliage, creating a dry zone down wind. While the wind breaking aspect of the trees is much appreciated, the moisture reducing properties of such a tree barrier are not. Succulents are the natural choice for such sites for gardeners wishing to reduce the cost and time involved in keeping up the almost constant supply of water needed to keep understorey plants thriving in these situations. Using succulents creates a harmonious balance few other plants can match.

Uneven ground with exposed tree roots, stumps, rocks or ground which cracks heavily is often difficult to cover with conventional plants. Mowing grass close to large trees or shrubs is often difficult with the mower blades hitting exposed roots or cutting into the ground. Succulents tolerate these conditions well and visually smooth out irregularities as well as covering cracked and unsightly ground. These places are great for small border succulent gardens, especially if sunny and exposed.

Aloe arborescens in dense shade under a large cypress.

Borders and driveways

The old fashion driveway which goes down the side of the house and along a neighbour's fence is often very neglected. Sometimes through frustration with gardening problems such areas are completely concreted over creating an ugly, bare and industrial-like landscape. But with a little foresight and the use of containerised succulents, an interesting, self-sustaining garden can be nurtured.

Older houses often have a driveway which is only partially concreted, having a soil or gravel covered middle strip. This was originally a way of reducing the unsightliness of oil spots, but with modern cars, oil spotting is much less of a problem. Why not plant low growing succulents in the area between the concrete wheel tracks? Often the driveway is only partially used anyway and it would greatly imporve the look of unsightly driveways. Succulents can be planted in patterns or designs which can be repeated for a tiling effect or can be totally abstract. The effect is only limited by your imagination!

Areas along or near fences

Almost every garden has a fence to deal with somewhere. Some make ideal gardening backdrops but others are liabilities, being too far away from watering points and from normal

A public park bench across the street from a hospital. As with the previous picture, here cotyledons are used for many reasons, one of which is their light reflectivity at dusk or at night.

At night, this *Cotyledon orbiculata* shines in the reflected light of a vehicle's headlights. Why not plant a clump on either side of your driveway for easy night-time navigation?

traffic flow. Fences next to where neighbours have a heavy tree population are usually hard to plant because of the root invasion from the trees.

Other difficult boundary areas include those on a slope where there is little or no soil along the fence line. Succulents can survive on as little as 50 mm of soil, which is much less than any other plant type. Low, wire fences can also be nicely landscaped with succulents where conventional shrubs would grow too high and block the view. Walls which serve as fences and consist of loose rock are ideal for succulents as these will grow on top of and in rock crevices. Concrete block fences are the most difficult to deal with but even these can be made less unsightly by either attaching pots or boxes and having hanging succulents tumbling down their sides.

Nature strips can be difficult to mow and water, especially when planted with trees having exposed roots. Note that the large trees on the adjoining property have drying and dead lawn.

New home owners might consider using alternative materials as fences which incorporate niches which can be filled with succulents and other hardy plants. Some concrete block styles designed as embankment retainers are admirably suited to planting with succulents (see photo page 36).

Country residents living in drier areas are often faced with ugly wire fencing in areas beyond the reach of hoses. These are usually planted with native shrubs which quickly become unsightly as well as creating a fire hazard and blocking the view. Succulents are a natural replacement as they add colour and, once established, survive without watering.

Succulents along rural borders
Succulents can be made into fences or used as boundary markers. The hardy tree jade (*Portulacaria afra*) can be trained and pruned to any shape (see page 75). At Lightning Ridge, central NSW, one property owner has used jade extensively as a fence-like barrier. Rural plantings of conifers which are fenced off from livestock can be heavily planted underneath the canopy where little else can survive. The silvery-white of *Cotyledon orbiculata* is a perfect candidate to brighten up windbreaks. *Cotyledon* species are poisonous to stock if eaten in quantity so use these with caution or plant them far enough away from a wire fence to prevent hungry stock from having a feed.

Focus and specimen succulent plants

The larger growing succulents make ideal focus plants in any garden. Because some attain considerable size, they should be placed in a position where they will not be a problem in later years. Careful research is required to find out how different species will eventually develop. Many will attain a large size and fill a substantial space within five or ten years. Correct placement at an early stage is therefore essential unless kept potted or restricted by a small soil area.

Advanced specimens of *Crassula ovata* (jade or money plant) look like miniature trees if grown in sufficient light. Once the lower branches have been pruned, the plants appear to be taller than they actually are. Since they are totally spineless and never grow too large, they can be placed close to paths or borders. If they require shifting they can be easily lifted and transplanted. As container plants they make ideal single pot specimens on decks, paved areas or around the pool area. While they do shed leaves as they mature, these are heavy and tend fall into the container rather than be blown about by the wind. *Portulacaria afra* can be treated in a similar manner but needs occasional pruning to maintain a compact form. Both species can withstand moderate frosts but suffer leaf damage when the temperature falls below -5°C.

The larger spine-tipped agaves (aside from *A. attenuata*) need to be placed further back in relation to traffic flow. Sometimes

Here a garden designer by the coast blends an assortment of native plants and local materials to create harmony in an otherwise bare, sandy, salt laden scene.

These cotyledons define the edges of this rustic set of steps. At night the cotyledons are also easy to see.

Yuccas come in a variety of sizes and leaf types. The spineless species are the most popular, with *Y. filamentosa* and *Y. flaccida* being the most commonly seen in the southern states. Both are short stemmed and have soft floppy leaves. The giant tree-like *Yucca elephantipes* grows to well over 5 m and can quickly become an imposing sight if grown in the garden. However, potted specimens will remain small and tidy. Most yuccas are difficult to shift once established so they need to be grown in their final position. The flowers of all yuccas are very similar, differing mostly in size and length of flower stalk. The fast growing spine-tipped yuccas are the vigorous *Y. aloifolia* and *Y. gloriosa*, both of which have rather sharp spined leaves and are best suited

spines are desired, such as under house windows to deter intruders, and in such situations agaves are highly recommended as they do not grow tall enough to block out sunlight yet provide a formidable looking barrier. Agaves, because of their bold leaves, look good when arranged with larger non-succulents with grass-like leaves such as *Doryanthus* (Gymea or spear lily) or *Phormium*.

Aloes, some of which have spines, can be arranged into a little group consisting of several different species, with the largest growing towards the back and the smaller ones in front. Many will flower annually, providing long lasting colour.

Write your own caption!

All the colours of the rainbow using succulent foliage alone.

their enormous flower spikes make this plant a worthwhile addition to the larger garden.

The Australian bottle tree (*Brachychiton rupestris*) is a good candidate for large gardens or for a showy giant pot. It is hardy, tolerating both heat and frost and will form a short tree with a bottle-like trunk. Trees can be kept in large pots which are ideal for decks because they tolerate drying wind and intermittent watering so much better than other trees.

In the true tropics the various species of *Adansonia* (baobob) can be grown but these need a large space as they almost all grow into large trees. Contact a specialist succulent nursery for further suggestions regarding large growing specimen succulents suitable for tropical situations.

Special uses

Raised beds

Raised beds are often constructed to give gardens more form and shape. They can be any shape and are usually made of masonry, concrete or wood. Raised beds are ideal for the elderly and those gardeners confined to wheelchairs. While we normally think of raised beds being only 200-300 mm in height, they can be constructed to be much higher and the tops can act as seating or staging for specimen pot plants. Raised beds tend to confine specimen plants to a size restricted by the container's dimensions, which is a major asset for those who want to keep potentially large growing plants in check.

to larger gardens along fence lines or along walls. The other uncommon yuccas are all spiny and slower growing than those mentioned above and are best suited to country gardens in inland areas as they withstand extreme temperatures well.

Dracaena draco is another good feature succulent with specimen potential for the larger garden. After growing to 2 m in height it will thicken in trunk, becoming a multi-branched tree with a very attractive shape. The leaves are spineless so the plants can be placed anywhere.

Doryanthus spp. are relatives of the agaves and are native to eastern Australia. Both are frost sensitive but most can withstand drought. The spineless strappy leaves and

Colour blocks

By this term we mean areas of the garden devoted to groupings of one species or repeated groupings of several species to give a mass effect within a short period of time. This technique has traditionally been used with annuals in a bedding display and with roses, but works equally well with many types of succulents. With succulents there is less work and they provide a longer lasting display. With succulents the desired effect comes from their coloured foliage and not from flowers, which are very seasonal. Colour blocks are effective on a slope, where the colours, leaf forms and textures can be most easily appreciated. Even small gardens can utilise colour blocks on a reduced scale. In most cases, the colour block technique is the only way to fill a garden within one season; however, plants need to be planted close together initially if the garden is to look at its very best quickly.

Rockeries

The traditional rockery often consists of a pile or slope of rocks planted with a mixture of plants that may or may not include cactus and succulents. This very old fashioned and limited view is a far cry from the great affects that rockeries can achieve today. An alternative way of looking at a rockery is to consider it the opposite of a ground cover, where the aim is to cover the soil with plants. In a rockery, much of the soil is covered by individual rocks, gravel or other hard material, with plants merely being the focus to a study

Bold statements and very creative design only take some imagination. Here both space and height are a consideration.

which aims at recreating a natural rocky out-crop. Each small rockery should have one focus plant and possibly several focus rocks. Alternatively, a Japanese style 'rock and gravel garden' can be the inspiration, with an area of raked white or red gravel as the fill area, while plants and rocks cover only a minority of the total area. Rockeries can be ordinary or inspiring and their successful creation depends greatly on the gardener's artistic and aesthetic ability and capacity to envision a finished product. The end result of planning will be much more pleasing than if odd plants are stuck here and there.

Problem trees

Shady places are traditionally thought of as a home for azaleas, hostas, fuchias and ferns. Unfortunately many shady places are created by trees which have roots in such abundance and of such efficiency that few plants can be maintained, much less thrive. Many gardeners have tried to plant annuals around the trunks of trees but this is almost always doomed to failure due to the dark conditions and a tree root system which quickly taps into any watered soil. In much of Victoria, cypresses (*C. macrocarpa*) are among the worst in this regard, providing heavy shade and keeping the soil virtually bone dry for most of the year. In the drier districts only the hardiest plants, such as English Ivy, can thrive under cypresses. Succulents, however, survive well under cypresses, and while not growing as strongly or as colourfully as those

This traditional rockery incorporates miniature alpines which grow among the smaller types of succulents.

(above) A simple bench with elegant potted succulents and seashells fills an odd corner of this garden.

From top: *Sedum rubrotinctum*, a sempervivum, *Echeveria* 'Violet Queen' and *Echeveria multicaulis*.

in a sunnier and wetter environment, they do brighten up otherwise dark and dreary spots. Other trees that can be a problem are pepper trees (*Shinus molle*), camphor laurel (*Cinnamonum camphora*), pines (*Pinus* spp.) and in fact almost any spreading tree that thrives and grows large.

Gardeners who are unlucky enough to have close neighbours with large spreading trees know what a chore it can be to grow plants successfully in areas riddled with tree roots. The heavy watering required to keep understorey plants alive only seems to make the offending trees grow faster. Such trees will actually extend and enlarge their root system in your garden in appreciation of your watering efforts. Other than digging a 600 mm trench along your fence line and filling it with steel sheets or concrete, there is no easy way to deny access to the invasive roots of problem trees. The easy solution is a succulent garden or at least a mixed understorey planting containing succulents.

Shady places

Heavily shaded locations in the inner city are another story. Buildings, high fences and mature trees combine to create difficult growing conditions for most types of small plants. Successful plant cultivation in shady environments requires careful plant selection, so seek expert advice on your particular situation. A few succulent groups will survive and grow well in half to full shade if the area is on the dry side. Gasterias, haworthias and some aloes can be considered (see page 88). If these fail, then gardeners may need to consider ferns or plastic plants!

Fire barriers

Most leaf succulents are nearly impossible to ignite. When used in broad beds or colour blocks they make excellent bushfire barriers. Unfortunately there is a misconception that all succulent leafed plants are equal in this regard. Several of the mesemb group are highly flammable when old and dry or stressed by drought. For security with living fire barriers, stick to the rosette and leaf succulent types such as echeverias, aeoniums, sedums, agaves and small aloes. To make a low fire-risk garden even safer, tidy up before the fire season begins, removing any dry plants, leaves and litter, including those which have blown in from elsewhere.

Erosion control

Steep banks and hillsides are becoming features of modern housing as suburbs advance up hillsides formerly covered in native bush. Often the soil at such sites is very thin and rocky. While builders usually bring in topsoil, it is often too thinly applied or too poor to support all but the hardiest plants. The choice is often between a native garden, with its associated fire hazard, straggly growth and untidiness, or a succulent and associated plants garden. Steep gardens will always be a problem. Some home owners delay planting steep banks because they think that they will eventually terrace, landscape, pave, extend, etc. but most of these ideas only come to

This concrete embankment retaining wall has been brightened up with a selection of succulents.

fruition once enough money becomes available. In the meantime, the slope becomes covered with a thin layer of weeds or is washed away by storm rains. The best alternative may be to quickly plant a stabilising cover of succulents which will at least hold the slope in place and protect it from weeds and erosion. The succulents can always be removed at a later date when funds are available for more permanent work. Succulents in the mesemb plant group grow well on very steep grades, including vertical walls.

Weed suppression

Weeds generally only grow well in places where they receive adequate light and moisture. Most succulents love the sun and will spread out their leaves to cover the ground fully. Succulents do not need supplementary

Cotyledon macrantha has been used to cover this once weedy area.

watering once established and this in itself suppresses weeds. Succulents compete with weeds for moisture supplied by rain, again reducing the capacity of weeds to grow vigorously. The key to weed suppression is a very dense covering of succulents and little or no added water and fertiliser. Weeds such as cape weed and winter grass, which seed annually, are the easiest to control in this manner, while perennial weeds such as couch grass may be more difficult to control. Oxalis, while tenacious, will be sorely tested by a dense succulent cover; however it is unlikely to be eliminated easily in areas which receive regular summer rain.

Weeds are often thick and difficult to extract because they have become entangled

among garden plants. With succulents this is not as much of a problem as is it far easier to gently pull out the succulents, spray the remaining weeds with herbicide and then replant the site two weeks later with the original succulents. The lifted succulents are fine when left to dry out of the ground for two weeks. Hand weeding will need to be carried out through the first season of any new succulent garden until it is fully established. Once they fill out, succulents are able to crowd out almost all weeds.

Holiday houses

Gardens around houses that are only visited occasionally during the year are ideal places for succulents, both in the open garden and in pots. Potted succulents can withstand

This bowls club in New Plymouth, New Zealand receives a high average annual rainfall. The club has used succulents to brighten up the top of their retaining wall. Little care and no watering is required.

many weeks without water, especially in coastal areas where temperatures are more equitable. Many aspects already discussed apply to the problem of maintaining plants and a garden around holiday houses.

Patios, decks and other non-soil areas

How often have you seen a planter or pot filled with dead or near-dead plants in someone's garden? It is usually not resting on the garden soil, where often the roots can penetrate into the soil, or the container is exposed to watering from sprinklers. Usually such plants are on hard surfaces where they are left and forgotten, especially when it comes to regular watering. In today's active and often away-from-home lifestyle, pot plants are under threat. Unless of course, they are succulents, most of which can survive in pots for months without any supplementary water. Not that they do not appreciate water during the heat and dry of summer; rather, they can survive the forgetfulness that a busy lifestyle can generate.

Wind is another aspect that areas such as decks and patios are exposed to. Often this can be severe, especially in coastal areas, and limits the choice of conventional plants to a handful, all of which still need frequent watering. While plants naturally lose water through their leaves and flowers, windy conditions increase water loss in plants by at least a factor of two, making regular watering even more essential. Again, succulents provide the answer. For more information on how to solve your outdoor container problems, see Chapter 4.

The pool

Pools are often landscaped with tropical looking foliage plants which is fine in the tropics where they grow well, but often results in slow growth in temperate zones. Palms are often favoured near pools, but as many people know, some species, such as the cotton palm, have hard leaves which can scratch or even injure those who carelessly brush by. While hibiscus bushes in flower look good, they do have an annoying habit of dropping old flowers and leaves, many of which fall into the pool. Most foliage trees and shrubs have similar problems to varying degrees. This means extra maintenance or an

unsightly pool. Splashed chlorinated or salt laden water from the pool can also damage many foliage plants. Areas near the pool planted with succulents will reduce the cleaning workload as well as create a different feel. To add to a pool's appeal, why not use occasional succulents near the waters edge? For something really different, surround the pool with a desert inspired landscape that will increase the pool's sense of coolness. Containers can also be kept inside the pool fence, reducing the caged and sterile look. Splashed water from the pool will not damage succulents as much as other foliage plants.

A simple yet elegant design using only a few flat rosette succulents.

Chapter 4

Containers

Mention balconies, terraces, decks, patios, porches and pool areas and most people will see plants in containers as part of their vision. A deck or terrace without containers filled with plants is unfinished and stark.

Container gardening, as here defined, is the growing of plants in moveable containers (pots, bowls, urns, barrels, laundry sinks and tubs). This differentiates container gardening from permanent planters such as the raised beds or fixed planter boxes often seen as features in large courtyards. Potted plants grow differently when given more room. Succulents grow far more quickly when in-ground or in large beds. A 200 mm tall ten year old potted plant can suddenly transform into a 600 mm tall specimen within a few months as a result of being released from the bondage of the pot. While this fast growth may be seen as positive, potted plants hold their shape and form better. They also have better colours and will be less brittle. And, of course, they can be easily moved and swapped around, allowing for a change in visual display at any time.

Container gardening offers many possibilities not available to those who only garden in the ground. Often container gardening is the only option for those in apartments who have only a balcony or small courtyard. Those who rent will also see the immediate advantage of container gardening: potted plants can be easily taken to a new location. Container gardening also offers the

Quality containers make even common plants a joy to look at. For sunny outdoor situations, succulents are easier to maintain in glazed ceramic or plastic containers as these do not dry out as quickly as terracotta. Succulents can be planted singly (above, with *Pachyphytum oviferum*) or massed as in the large glazed urn below.

ability to change the scene easily. A new look can be quickly created by moving containers. While some gardens will only consisit of containers, most will have a combination of ground plantings and containers, which together complete the ideal garden scene. Containers are most practical near high traffic areas such as paths and doorways. In larger groupings, the barbecue and entertainment areas are also ideal for containers because these areas are near water sources and can be given a higher level of care than the general garden. High traffic areas should have highly visual plants. These can be plants which flower for long periods (very rare!) or, like succulents, have stylish and colourful foliage. Succulents provide year-round foliage, colour and contrast.

(above) Tree stumps in the garden can be turned into interesting features by planting them with echeverias. Alternatively, hollow logs can be used as plant containers. (below) A plastic pot, but the setting creates atmosphere.

When compared to outdoor grown plants, containerised succulents have a greater need for protection from extremes of heat and cold. The temperature in pots will vary greatly during sunny days. Moisture and nutrient levels will also vary much more widely than they do for ordinary in-ground plants. All of these factors stress potted plants, but with succulents this often results in more attractive and compact growth as well as excellent leaf colouration.

Another great aspect about succulents in containers is that they are so collectable. Cactus and succulent collections can be general or specialise in a few types, some of which are ideal for sunny window-sills. With over 4000 different species to choose from, there is plenty of scope for the collector's urge to find just the right group.

(above) Ceramic pots and bowls come in a variety of sizes and shapes and, with proper foresight, can set off and complement the succulents they contain.
(below) The large elegant bowl below complements this mixed planting of succulents and would be an ideal feature for a sunny home entry.

Containers come in a wide variety of sizes and materials. Weight may be a consideration for those wishing to grow in larger containers. The choice is usually between ceramics and plastics, which in the larger sizes are often equally priced. Quality plastic containers can be more expensive than cheap ceramics, but if portability is a consideration then plastic is the better option. Succulents grow better in plastic or glazed ceramic pots than in unglazed terracotta ones. While the terracotta look is attractive, rapid water loss through the pot walls results in plants growing very slowly or not at all. Staining and eventual salting up of the pot surface is another drawback of terracotta. Some terracotta pots are glazed on the inside and these, as well as all other glazed ceramic pots, are better suited to the majority of succulents

Landscape designers are using succulents in the most modern of garden designs. Note that the raised beds have drainage holes near the centre of the picture.

because they will not dry out as rapidly. Unglazed terracotta can be painted on the inside with clear or coloured plastic-based finishes such as polyurethane varnishes or acrylic paints.

Western red cedar or treated pine (either natural, stained or textured) is suitable for containers. An advantage with wood is that those with the tools and time can construct their own containers to fit their special sites.

Other container materials range from recycled agricultural plough discs, upended concrete pipe sections, old wine barrels, tubs, concrete blocks and concrete cast pots to bizarre but functional items such as old bathtubs, sinks and recycled vehicle tyres.

While the latter items may not be everyone's idea of good taste, they open up possibilities for the use of other recyclable containers.

Window boxes are very underused in Australia and can easily brighten up an ordinary house facade. Succulents are ideally suited to window boxes, especially those facing north and west. As window box plants, succulents can withstand several seasons without being moved, unlike other plants which usually need to be changed seasonally. Other plants soon suffer in window boxes, and while annuals look great when in full flower, one weekend away during hot weather can turn them into composting candidates. Inner city gardens and Victorian houses look good with window boxes but many newer houses can use them to distract us from the starkness of brick and glass.

Older weatherboard houses can have pot hangers easily fitted to the windowsills, which allows flexibility of view because pots can be rotated. Window boxes need not be filled with potting mix; instead, smaller pots can be arranged in them and changed to suit mood or season. This has the advantage of insulating the pot from extreme heat while also keeping it from drying out too quickly. Houses with outdoor stairs may wish to use 'stair boxes' that sit on the margins of the treads or are fixed to wide railings.

Balconies are often overloaded with a hodgepodge of pots of different sizes, colours and materials. While this may please the owner, it has very little aesthetic appeal.

This rooftop garden design won a Gold Medal at the Melbourne International Flower and Garden Show in 1999.

An investment in quality containers of a similar material and colour will improve your view as well as that from the street. Succulents are far and away the best plants for sunny balconies, especially for people who are on the go and away from home for extended periods. Balcony containers will look best if planted up with only one group of plants such as succulents. Not only is maintenance easier, but it gives the containers on the balcony a sense of unity.

Rooftop gardens are a new concept for most home owners. While the traditional Australian home with its tile roof is unsuitable for rooftop gardens, the trend towards inner city living opens up many sites in condominiums, lofts and converted industrial buildings which are suitable for roof gardening. Because succulents need only a small

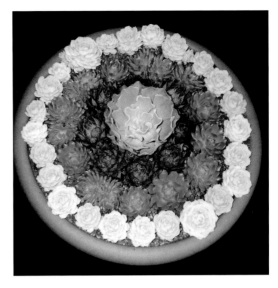

(above) Simple symmetry can be very effective. Here echeverias are tightly arranged by colour and size. (below) Wooden planter boxes, which are now ready to hang on a wall like small paintings. Grown permanently like this they need more care with watering. Home-made containers can be constructed from untreated or treated timber.

A collection of mostly potted echeverias. The intense colouration of these plants indicates that they have been grown under high light intensity and low fertiliser levels.

volume of potting mix for their survival, they can be used without fear of exceeding the engineered load of the roof. Succulents also have shallow roots that will never damage a roof's structure if planted in shallow garden beds on rooftops. Because of the low water requirements, the risk of water damage through rooftop irrigation is also minimised. Succulents also tolerate extreme wind, giving them another plus. Naturally, pots and other containers on roofs should be made of plastic or wood and a lightweight potting mix should be chosen.

Succulent bowls planted up as 'gardens' are a source of enjoyment for many. These can be made up for instant impact by planting them with larger, mature plants or they can be planted with small plants which will eventually grow to fill all the spaces. The lat-

ter is an ideal children's project that will teach them about propagation, care, growth and plant requirements.

Dark interiors are not suitable for containerised succulents; however, their form and colour can still be enjoyed indoors. Why not try low or shallow bowls planted with succulents as a decorative alternative to a vase of flowers or a bowl of fruit on a coffee table or bench indoors? Many succulents in dark situations quickly fade in colour and elongate, so only keep your containers indoors for a few days before returning them to their outdoor growing situations.

Requirements for successful container gardening with succulents

A site receiving several hours of direct sun is ideal for succulents in containers. The more sun the better for most species, but there are several types which grow happily in bright light without any direct sunlight. draughty sites are preferred over protected sites. Succulents will generally not grow in places favoured by ferns and mosses. As a general rule, the more sun and exposure to the elements the better succulents will look and perform.

Once the container is chosen, the type of potting mix needs to be considered. The purpose of repotting is to replace worn-out 'soil' as well as to provide space for new growth. Any reputable potting mix is suitable for most of the succulents covered in this book. Special cactus mixes are available and these are also recommended; however, they are not recommended for most succulents. Crocking drainage holes (filling the bottom of the pot with stones or gravel) is totally unnecessary. Plants which are purchased in pots should be unpotted and have their root ball slightly broken up. This will stimulate the plant to produce new roots. To repot, place the bare-rooted plants into new potting mix to the desired height in the pot and fill in the space between the roots with additional mix. Containers should be filled to just below full capacity without applying any compaction, as pressing down on the potting mix reduces the air spaces. The more air spaces in the mix, the better the air to water ratio when the potting mix is wet. A light and fluffy potting mix will grow better plants than a compacted one. Replanting tall specimens can be a problem as they will have a tendency to tip over in loose potting mix and it is preferable to temporarily stake the plant upright as opposed to heavily compacting around the roots. Alternatively, rocks or other removable objects can be temporarily stacked up against the stems to keep them upright until they stand firmly on their own.

Birdbaths make novel yet tasteful pots. Avoid planting only a few widely spaced plants in large containers as this will look sparse and lack the luxuriant look of a fully planted container such as this one.

Part 2
Succulent Library

This section of the book contains photographs of many of our favourite succulents (arranged alphabetically) which are suitable for Australian gardens. Since a book of this size could never fully illustrate all of the succulents suitable for gardens, we have included only a few representative plants which best show the whole group's features. Additional information is given in the appendix about features that may not be obvious from the photographs or captions. Check with your local cactus and succulent society (see page 95 for details) who may be able to help you with information on obtaining less common succulents.

Aeoniums

All aeoniums have flat rosettes with relatively thin leaves. Aeoniums originate from the Canary Islands where they experience winter rainfall and dry summers. They are at their best in coastal gardens but can withstand the harsh conditions of inland areas, especially if the summers are not too humid. Growth is mostly from autumn through to spring. Aeoniums can withstand light or even moderate frosts and will grow in shady locations. Many species have showy yellow flowers. There are at least twenty-five species as well as many hybrids like the popular A. 'Zwartkop', which was named in Holland.

Flowers of most aeoniums are produced during winter and make a colourful display in any garden situation.

(below) An *Aeonium* showing summer colours.

(upper left) *Aeonium arboreum*.
(left) *Aeonium tabuliforme*, also known as the "plate plant".
It grows to 300 mm as a smooth stemless flat disk.
(lower left) *Aeonium 'Zwartkop'* (also known as *A.
'Schwartzkopf'* or *A. 'Swartzkop'*).
(above) The variegated *Aeonium decorum* 'Tricolor'.
(below) This variegated aeonium prefers some shade.

Agaves

Agaves range in size from miniature fit-in-your-hand types to giants weighing several tonnes when mature. Most species have thick leaves with sharp terminal spines. Full sun, wind and high summer temperatures are tolerated by all species. Most can withstand severe frosts. Agaves originate from North America where they occupy habitats ranging from true deserts to mountainous pine and oak forests. Agaves have a somewhat bad reputation because of one species, *A. americana*, which has naturalised itself in some parts of Australia. This species has little horticultural merit when compared to the wealth of beautiful and well behaved species now available commercially.

(above) *Agave stricta* forms tight multi-leafed spheres.
(below) *A. filifera* is one of several thread-edged species.
(opposite top left) *Agave victoriae-reginae* forms compact rosettes and tolerates frost well.
(opposite top right) Leaf impressions on *A. parrasana*.
(opposite lower left) *A. parrasana* is a small growing and non-invasive species suitable for all garden sizes.

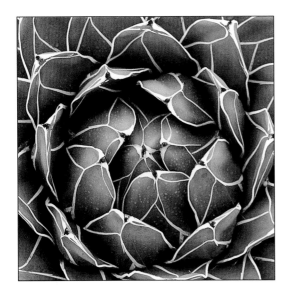

Aloes

Aloes are mostly native to Africa where at least 300 species have been recorded. They occupy habitats ranging from wet and cool temperate regions to tropical deserts, so there will be several species suitable for any area of Australia. In size, they vary from thimble size to small trees. Aloes flower freely with red being the most common colour. Most flower in winter but there are species that flower during every month of the year.

(left) Several *Aloe* species grow to the size of a small tree. Most will flower during winter.
(below) *Aloe* x *spinosissima*. This compact hybrid is very popular. It flowers readily in spring even when quite young. The leaves look fierce but are soft to the touch, making it good for public places (see page 11).

(above) *Aloe ferox* flowers are attractive to birds.
(above right) The *Aloe* 'saponaria' group contains a number of species with spotted or flecked leaves.
(right) An assortment of aloes.
(lower right) *Aloe ferox*.
(below) *Aloe variegata* is usually seen as an indoor pot plant but does well in gardens.

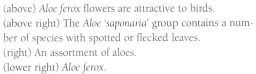

Bromeliads (terrestrial)

Several genera of bromeliads are seen in gardens. Puyas are a large growing group. They often form sizeable clumps and are mostly characterised by having silvery recurved leaves. They have spines along their leaf edges and are best used away from traffic areas. As backdrops to smaller succulents, puyas make a hardy and showy addition to larger gardens. Aechmeas and dyckias are smaller growing bromeliads, forming tidy clumps with age. Terrestrial bromeliads do best in full sun throughout Australia.

(upper left) *Dyckia marnier-lapostollei* grows to 300 mm.
(left) *Aechmea recurvata* is a very hardy species.
(below) Assorted garden hardy varieties which prefer dry and sunny positions.

Cactus

We have chosen only a few of the thousands of cactus species which are hardy yet make a dramatic statement in any garden. The species shown can stand both winter and summer rainfall and also tolerate regular frosts. For those who like the look of cactus, there is a wealth of other species that will thrive in almost any garden situation.

(right) Different forms of *Cereus peruvianus*. Note the large red edible fruits.
(below) One of the many species of *Mammillaria*.
(bottom left) *Parodia (Notocactus) leninghausii* forms attractive clumps and has soft spines.
(bottom right) A selection of different opuntias.

Cotyledons

A small group of shrubby succulents from South Africa. Several have a white wax covering on their leaves, giving them a silvery sheen. The commonly available species reach 400 mm in height and are fast growers. They do not like summer humidity as they are then susceptible to moulds. Cotyledons can be poisonous to livestock. Cotyledons do particularly well in areas receiving winter rainfall. They can tolerate some frost.

(left) *Cotyledon orbiculata* in flower during autumn. Behind is the closely related wavy leafed form 'Silver Waves'.
(below) *Cotyledon tomentosa* is a small growing species which develops attractive furry brown leaf tips when grown in sunny locations.

(above and below) *Cotyledon macrantha*. Note how the plant below, which is growing in full sunlight has not been recently fertilised, has developed intense leaf edge colouration.

(right) *Cotyledon orbiculata* 'Silver Waves' quickly grows to 400 mm in height.

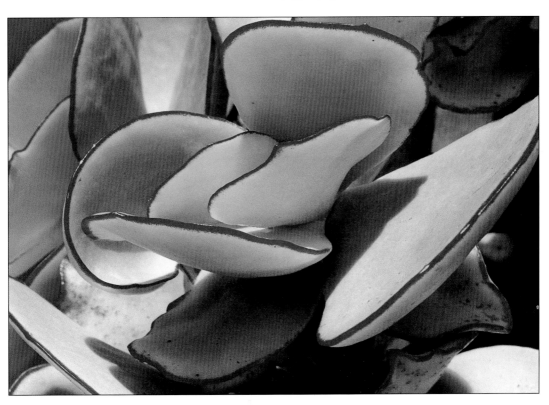

Crassulas

The most commonly seen crassulas are thick stemmed shrubs which can reach 1 m in height. They are ideal for larger gardens or as specimen pot plants in large tubs. Most species are dainty gems which are best suited to small pots or to courtyards and verandas, where their jewel-like foliage can best be appreciated. Use the larger ones as backdrops to smaller succulents and plant the smaller growing species along paths where their foliage will not be overgrown.

(left) The compact form of *Crassula ovata* with the bluish leafed *Crassula arborescens*. Both species make excellent bonsai candidates.
(lower left) *Crassula* 'Baby's Necklace' flowers.
(lower right) *Crassula ovata* 'Hummel's Sunset'

(above) *Crassula falcata* is unusual in producing intense red flowers during spring and autumn.

(right) *Crassula* 'Hobbit' (also known as *C.* 'Gollum' or *C.* 'Green Coral') forms low mounds. It is one of the many forms of *Crassula ovata*.

(below) The shrubby *Crassula* 'Hummel's Sunset' and *C. arborescens* both provide unusual foliage colours for gardens or pots.

Echeverias (small types)

Echeverias are mostly rosette forming with a tendency to form clumps of several heads in a few years. Most of the smaller echeverias grow no taller than 150 mm. Colours and shapes can vary slightly with the seasons, with autumn and winter being the time for best leaf colouration. After flowering, remove dead or dry flower stalks. Smaller echeverias enjoy being replanted regularly.

(above) *E.* 'Black Prince' showing young flower buds. If stressed, plants turn almost black.
(below) *Echeveria secunda*, and *Echeveria* 'Violet Queen'. Both of these are matched in size and growth habit, allowing them to be used together effectively in long term bedding displays where consistency is desired.
(right) From left, *E. globulosa*, *E.* 'Perle von Nurnburg' and *E.* 'Black Prince'.
(lower right) *E. lilacina* and *E.* 'Afterglow' (larger pot).

(above) *Echeveria agavoides*. This form is displaying beautiful summer colours. In shade the red may fade.
(left) The superb varieties and colours of echeverias available today are absolutely magnificent.
(below) Highly coloured echeverias provide stunning colour spots among ordinary garden plants.

Echeverias
(large frilly and fancy types)

These echeverias are mostly frilly or wavy along their outer leaf edges. They are all rosette forming and flower freely with tall flower spikes. While some echeverias such as *E. imbricata* produce copious offsets, most of the better varieties are less spreading. Many of the fancy leafed types never produce offsets; instead they grow tall with age and may need to have their 'head' cut off and replanted. Avoid fertilising echeverias as this produces lanky and weak growth.

(This page and opposite) A selection of some of the many frilly and fancy leafed *Echeveria* hybrids now available. Most are best suited to pots which can be sheltered from the worst of the winter or wet weather.

Euphorbias

Euphorbias are mostly perennials and are very diverse. Most species are very cactus-like; however, several are spineless and make wonderful additions to low-water-use gardens. While most species have greenish flowers, reds and oranges are also available. Almost all euphorbias have milky sap in their stems and leaves which runs freely when the plant is scratched or cut. This milky sap is caustic to sensitive skin and eyes so be careful when handling plants. Always wear gloves!

(left) *Euphorbia milii* comes in a variety of sizes and flower colours. Plants grow best in the subtropics. (below) *Euphorbia rigida* is a very good performer with very bright yellow flower heads in winter turning reddish brown lasting all through spring and early summer.

(above) *Euphorbia myrsinites* is a sprawling perennial which grows to 500 mm. Try one in a hanging pot.(Photo C. Blazey)
(below) *Euphorbia flanaganii* forms an almost cushion-like mound of soft finger-like tentacles. Good for borders.

Graptopetalums and their hybrids

Graptopetalums are mostly dwarf rosetted leaf succulents that display beautiful pastel colours. Most species are native to steep and cool mountain regions of Mexico. While many members are essentially stemless, some, such as *Graptopetalum paraguayense*, develop long stems which can add character to many garden situations.

A number of *Graptopetalum* species have been hybridised with other related genera to form new plants which combine the best features of their parents. Graptoverias are bred from crossings with echeverias.

(above) *Graptopetalum bellum*, also known as *Tacitus bellus*, is a miniature species which flowers for weeks just before Christmas. It is best grown in pots.
(below right) *Graptopetalum bellum* has two flower forms. The more commonly seen pink form has larger flowers and stronger growth.
(below) *Graptopetalum superbum*.

(above) *Graptoveria* 'Silver Star' forms compact rosettes with hair-like leaf tips. It will form clumps in time.
(right) A *Graptoveria* growing among geraniums.
(below) *Graptoveria* 'Debbie' provides stunning pinkish-purple colouration in any succulent garden arrangement.

Kalanchoes

Kalanchoes are a very diverse group ranging in size from small ground covers to the large and sculptural tree-like *K. beharensis*. Most species are native to Madagascar. Most kalanchoes are not very frost tolerant. They are ideal for tropical and subtropical gardens, where they can withstand hot and humid summer conditions as well as high rainfall. Selected forms of *K. blossfeldiana* are frequently sold during winter as flowering indoor plants.

(left) *Kalanchoe pumila* is a miniature species with silver-gray foliage. The flowers are produced in spring.
(below) One of the many forms of *Kalanchoe beharensis*. Many types can grow to well over 1 m and make excellent and spectacular backdrops to lower growing succulents.

(above) *Kalanchoe fedtschenkoi* showing summer colours.
(upper right) *Kalanchoe marmorata* leaves show attractive markings, especially when stressed.
(lower right) *Kalanchoe blossfeldiana* comes in a variety of flower colours. The hardier types are suitable for sheltered outdoor situations.
(below) *K. tomentosa*, also known as the panda plant.

Mesembs

Mesembs, short for mesembryanthemums, belong to a large family of mostly low growing South African leaf succulents. Most are suitable for the garden only and can spread quickly to fill large areas. They can be contained to a smaller area if pruned regularly. Most common species are grown as ground covers and for their carpet-like flowering in spring, but there is a wide selection of other types which come in many forms and colours.

(upper left) *Lampranthus* displaying an almost irresistible show of shiny, vivid daisy-like flowers which carpet the ground during spring.
(left) The amazing colour intensity of a mesemb flower.
(right) *Drosanthemum speciosum* flowers in spring.
(lower right) Close-up of a *Cheiridopsis* species.
(below) *Oscularia deltoides*.

Other succulents

There are hundreds of other, less common succulents which have garden plant potential. We have illustrated a few below but we recommend that you experiment with other succulents not mentioned. Let us know how you get along!

Further information on the less common succulents can be obtained from the texts mentioned on page 95.

(left) *Pachypodium lamerei* naturally grows like a standard with a bare understorey. Where there are no frosts it will flower with almost frangipani-like flowers which have a heavenly perfume to match.
(lower left) The Queensland bottle tree (*Brachychiton rupestris*) fits well into larger succulent gardens. Naturally a dwarf tree, it can be pruned to any shape or size. In the background is a *Furcraea* sp. while the foreground shows one of the many perennial non-succulent euphorbias which put on long-lasting spring flower displays.
(below) *Lewisia* hybrids come in a wide variety of flower colours. While they have succulent leaves, they require more water and some shade during mid-summer to look their best.

(above) *Othonna capensis* is a low growing leaf succulent which spreads quickly by rooting along its trailing stems. (left) Both native Australian *Doryanthus* species fit well into larger succulent landscapes. Their long lasting and spectacular flower spikes brighten up any garden. (Photo J. Sutherland)

(below) For those gardeners with a sense of the grand, *Nolina gracilis* and the related *Nolina recurvata* ('Ponytail palm') make stunning additions to the large garden.

(above) Haworthias are mostly shade loving.
(right) Furcraeas are fast growing succulents which look
fierce but are actually soft leafed and without spines.
(below) *Dracaena draco* eventually grows into a large
multi-branched tree. Here, it grows with aeoniums and
Phormium. Behind it are two mature *Yucca elephantipes*.

(above) Gasterias come in a variety of sizes and are useful for shady places.
(left) The flowers of the yucca-like *Hesperaloe parviflora* are on 1 m tall spikes. Flowers are produced all summer.
(below) *Portulaca afra* is used here as a hedge and a screen. Often called 'jade', it comes in several different leaf colour forms.

Pachyphytums
and their hybrids

This frost hardy group of succulents is characterised by having chunky leaves and small rosettes. They are neat and compact growers, usually only 100-250 mm in diameter and are ideal for pots and small places in the garden. Full sun is required for them to exhibit their best colour and growth. There are a number of hybrids of *Pachyphytum* species crossed with echeverias.

(left) *Pachyveria* 'Elaine Wright' has wax coated leaves. Here, it contrasts well with *Sedum nussbaumeranum*.
(below) *Pachyphytum compactum* has slightly angular wax covered leaves.
(upper right) This hardy crested *Pachyphytum* x *Echeveria* hybrid forms compact bluish mounds.
(lower right) *Pachyphytum oviferum* has the common name of 'sugar almonds'.

Sedums

A very diverse group of succulents which is composed mostly of species suitable for ground covers. There are also some shrubby species, some of which can grow up to 1 m in height. Some excellent flowering types can be found, many of which attract butterflies. The sedums include some true miniatures such as *S. dasyphyllum,* which has mature heads only 10 mm across.

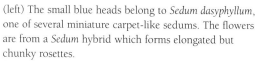

(left) The small blue heads belong to *Sedum dasyphyllum,* one of several miniature carpet-like sedums. The flowers are from a *Sedum* hybrid which forms elongated but chunky rosettes.
(lower left) *Sedum clavatum* forms small mounds and is very frost hardy.
(below) *Sedum sieboldii* on sprawling stems, making it an ideal hanging basket specimen for sunny locations.

(above and upper right) Flowering in spring, *Sedum* 'Vera Jamison' develops rich burgundy foliage. (Photos C. Blazey) (below) *Sedum pachyphyllum* has bluish leaves which are red tipped when the plant is stressed by intense sunlight and lack of fertiliser. It is growing with *Sedum rubrotinctum*. Both species make good ground covers and are useful in colour blocks.

Sedums continued

(left) The leaf colours on *Sedum nussbaumeranum* provide wonderful contrast. This plant was formerly *Sedum adolfii*
(above) *Sedum* 'Burrito' is useful for hanging baskets.
(below) *Sedum spectabile* 'Autumn Joy' attracts butterflies.

Senecios

Even though there are many succulent senecios, only a few are widely seen in the garden. Two blue leafed species are commonly seen and often misidentified. *Senecio mandraliscae* has bluish pencil-thick leaves that always point upwards. It has small white flowers and can spread into large but low clumps over several years. *Senecio serpens* looks like a dwarf version of *S. mandraliscae*. Its leaves are only 20-50 mm long and it forms smaller and much more compact clumps. It has a clumping habit whereas *S. mandraliscae* will trail with age. There are a number of lesser known succulent senecios which may occasionally be found in nurseries or in succulent collections.

(above) *Senecio petraea*, also known as *S. jacobsenii*, has trailing stems which can become purple in intense sunlight. Here, it grows with a miniature *Crassula* species.
(lower left) *Senecio serpens*.
(below) *Senecio mandraliscae*.

Sempervivums

All are small to medium sized rosette succulents which form compact clumps composed of several to many heads. They are native to the European mountains and are able to tolerate frosts and even snow. Historically known as 'house leeks' or 'live-forevers' for their ability to grow on roofs without soil, they have recently been rediscovered by herbalists for their curative properties. All species have very shallow roots and show good colour development in very poor soils.

(left) *Sempervivum tectorum* growing among rocks.
(below) Sempervivums come in a variety of colours.
(right) Typical *Sempervivum* flowers.
(far right) Leaves showing seasonal colour changes.
(lower right) Three *Sempervivum* species showing different growth forms. Smaller growing species often cluster.

Yuccas

Some yuccas have soft tipped leaves but most species have a terminal spine. All have lance-like leaves that radiate out like swords from the centre of the plant. The flowers are produced on tall spikes and consist of large, cup-shaped flowers in either white or cream. Most species are extremely hardy to frost, hail or snow, and tolerate drought. Several species become branched trees.

(left) Flowers of *Yucca filamentosa* (also below.
(below) *Yucca filamentosa* and *Y. flaccida* look very alike.
(opposite upper right) The soft leafed *Yucca "desmitiana"* grows to only 1 m in height.
(opposite upper left) Mature *Yucca brevifolia* growing as a street tree.
(opposite lower right) A flowering *Yucca aloifolia*.
(opposite lower left) The leaves of a variegated form of *Yucca aloifolia*. This species quickly grows to 2 m.

Names

Common name and synonyms	Correct botanical name
Aloe barbadensis	*Aloe vera*
Beaucarnea recurvata	*Nolina recurvata*
Black rose	*Aeonium arboreum* 'Zwartkop'
Century plant	*Agave* species
Christmas star	*Graptopetalum bellum*
Crassula argentea	*Crassula ovata*
Dragon's blood	*Dracaena draco*
Echeveria glauca	*Echeveria imbricata*
Echeveria secunda	*Echeveria glauca* var. *pumila*
Elephant's foot	*Dioscorea elephantipes*
Felt plant	*Kalanchoe beharensis*
Good luck plant	*Crassula ovata*
Hen and chickens	*Echeveria glauca* var. *pumila*
Hen and chickens	*Sempervivum* (clumping)
House leeks	*Sempervivum* (clumping)
Ice plant	*Dorotheanthus bellidoniformis*
Jade tree	*Portulacaria afra*
Jade tree (giant form)	*Crassula ovata*
Jaws	*Faucaria* species
Jelly bean plant	*Sedum pachyphyllum* and *S. rubrotinctum*
Livingstone daisy	*Dorotheanthus bellidoniformis*
Madagascar palm	*Pachypodium lamerei* and *P. geayi*
Mesembryanthemum criniflorus	*Dorotheanthus bellidoniformis*
Mesembryanthemum crystallinum	*Dorotheanthus bellidoniformis*
Money tree	*Crassula ovata*
Pigface	*Lampranthus* and *Carpobrotus* species
Pigface	Several other related genera
Plate/saucer plant	*Aeonium tabuliforme*
Ponytail palm	*Nolina recurvata*
Propeller plant	*Crassula falcata*
Queen agave	*Agave victoriae-reginae*
Red edge (cotyledon)	*Cotyledon macrantha*
Sedum adolphii	*Sedum nussbaumeranum*
Senecio serpens	*Senecio mandriliscae*
Silver waves	*Cotyledon orbiculata* (wavy leafed form)
Sugar almonds	*Pachyphytum oviferum*

Succulent growth forms

There are as many shapes and sizes as there are different types of succulents. The tables below gives an indication of average sizes. Note that not all of those in the first column are suitable as bedding plants as they may be too slow, expensive or rare, or have non-clumping features. See the table on page 88 for recommended ground covers.

Low growing or bedding plants
usually 50-300 mm tall

Abromeitiella species
Aeonium tabuliforme
Agave parviflora
Aloe brevifolia
Aloe aristata
Aloe mitriformis
Aloe saponaria
Aloe somaliensis
Aloe spinosissima
Aloe variegata
Crassula anomala
Crassula falcata
Crassula 'Gollum'
Crassula 'Jade Necklace' *
Crassula (most species)
Delosperma cooperi
Dorotheanthus species
Echeveria species
Euphorbia flanaganii
Faucaria species
Gasteria species
Graptopetalum species
Haworthia species
Kalanchoe blossfeldiana
Kalanchoe marmorata
Kalanchoe tomentosa
Lampranthus species
Oscularia deltiodes *
Pachyphytum species
Sedum acre
Sedum dasyphyllum
Sedum nussbaumerianum *
Sedum pachyphyllum *
Sedum reflexum *
Sedum rubrotinctum *
Sedum rubrotinctum var. 'Aurora'
Sedum sieboldii *
Sedum spathulifolia
Sedum spurium
Sedum variegatum
Sedum 'Vera Jameson' *
Sedum (most dwarf varieties)
Sempervivum species
Senecio petrea (S. jacobsenii) *
Senecio mandriliscae

Shrubs or specimens
usually 300-900 mm tall

Adenia obesum
Aeonium species
Agave decipiens
Agave filifera
Agave americana var. mediopicta
Agave parrasana
Agave parryi
Agave potatorum
Agave stricta
Agave victoriae-reginae
Aloe vera (A. barbadensis)
Aloe distans
Aloe gariepensis
Aloe microstigma
Aloe striata
Aloe vera
Cotyledon macrantha
Cotyledon orbiculata
Cotyledon 'Silver Waves'
Crassula ovata
Crassula arborescens
Dioscorea elephantipes
Dyckia species
Euphorbia caput-medusae *
Euphorbia horridus
Euphorbia mammillaris
Ficus petiolaris
Hesperaloe parviflora
Kalanchoe diagramontianum
Kalanchoe fedtschenkoi
Kalanchoe tubiflora
Portulacaria afra (green)
Portulacaria afra (gold)
Puya species
Ruschia species
Sedum dendroideum ssp. praealtum
Sedum spectabile
Sedum spectabile 'Autumn Joy'
Senecio mandriliscae
Yucca "desmetiana"
Yucca filamentosa
Yucca whipplei

Large specimens, shrubs or tree-like
1-2 m tall

Agave americana
Agave atrovirens
Agave attenuata
Agave ferdinandi-regis
Agave 'Grey Ghost'
Alluaudia procera
Aloe arborescens
Aloe bainesii
Aloe dichotoma
Aloe ferox
Aloe marlothii
Aloe plicatilis
Cussonia species
Dasylirion wheeleri
Dracaena draco
Euphorbia lambii
Furcraea species
Kalanchoe beharensis
Nolina recurvata
Nolina stricta
Pachypodium geayi
Pachypodium lamerei
Yucca species (most)

Trailing ground covers

Aptenia species *
Carpobrotus species (African)
Mossia intervallensis (a mesemb)
Melephora species (a mesemb)
Othonna capensis

Native Australian succulents

Carpobrotus glaucescens (trailing habit)
Carpobrotus rossii (trailing habit)
Disphyma crassifolium (trailing habit)
Adansonia gregorii (a tropics-only tree)
Brachychiton rupestris (small tree)

The symbol * represents recommended plants for hanging baskets.

Shady places

Though many succulents may survive and even grow in shade, most will not look as good as they could, or should, turning pale and weak with time. Below are those that grow well in shade.

Very shady

Aeonium tabuliforme
Aloe mitriformis
Aloe saponaria
Aptenia (may not flower well)
Echeveria glauca var. *pumila*
Haworthias (all species)
Gasterias (all species)

Semi-shade

Agave americana
Cotyledons (all species)
Echeverias, most (except pinks and whites)
Sansevieria species
Sempervivums
Plus all of the 'very shady' list above.

Several exquisite succulent *Kalanchoe* species, such as the one pictured below, can be very weedy, especially in tropical areas. Check with your local council for advice.

Recommended ground covers

These succulents are fast growing and clumping in habit and have been selected from the list of low growing succulents on page 86. All of these can be planted with an average spacing of 150-200 mm apart, but can be planted closer together for a quicker effect. (∗ exceptions see below.)

Aptenia ∗ (fast growing with trailing habit)
Carpobrotus ∗ (fast growing with trailing habit)
Chasmatophyllum species
Dorotheanthus bellidiformis (annual)
Echeveria elegans
Echeveria glauca var. *pumila*
Echeveria 'Violet Queen'
Lampranthus (all species) ∗ (Can quickly spread to 1 metre.)
Mesembryanthemum (all species, annuals)
Oscularia deltiodes ∗ (Can quickly spread to 1 metre.)
Portulaca (annuals)
Sedum acre
Sedum nussbaumeranum
Sedum pachyphyllum
Sedum reflexum
Sedum rubrotinctum
Sedum spathulifolium
Sedum spurium
Sempervivum species
Senecio mandraliscae
Senecio serpens (*S. repens*)

Coastal locations

This includes salt laden windy areas where many other plant types seldom thrive. Below is a list of highly recommended and well proven succulents for such locations.

Species	Plant colours
Aeoniums	greens, purples, blacks
Aloes (most)	greens, purples, browns
Aptenias	rich green
Carpobrotus	green (trailing)
Cotyledons	greens and silver-greys
Echev. imbricata	metal blue-grey
Lampranthus	(flowers of mixed colours)
Senecio serpens	blue
S. mandraliscae	blue
Shrubby sedums	mostly green

Frost tolerance

This can vary a lot depending on plant age, size and the level and regularity of frost. The plants below are very hardy.

Agave americana (except *medio-picta*)

Aloe arborescens

Aloe broomii

Aloe mitriformis

Aloe saponaria

Dasylirion (all species)

Echeveria imbricata

Echeveria glauca var. *pumila*

Euphorbia flanaganii

Faucaria species

Furcraea species

Nolina recurvata

Sempervivums

Yuccas (most species)

Best for pots

All succulents can and will grow in pots. Those listed below are exceptional examples worth considering.

50-300 mm size

Aloe somaliensis

Aloe variegata

Crassula 'Gollum'

Crassula 'Hobbit'

Sempervivum 'Oddity'

Echeveria species

Faucaria species

Kalanchoe blossfeldia hybrids

Kalanchoe pumila

Pachyphytum species

Sempervivum species

300-900 mm size

Aeonium 'Zwartkop'

Agave stricta var. *nana*

Agave titanota

Agave victoriae-reginae

Aloe melanacantha

Crassula ovata

Dioscorea elephantipes

Euphorbia horrida

Euphorbia mammillaris

Ficus petiolaris

Taller growing

Agave attenuata

Aloe dichotoma

Aloe ferox

Aloe plicatilis

Dracaena draco

Kalanchoe beharensis

Nolina recurvata

Pachypodium geayi

Pachypodium lamerei

Yucca elephantipes

Succulents suitable for humid or tropical climates

50-300 mm size
Kalanchoe (dwarf forms)
Sedum nussbaumeranum
Senecio serpens

300-900 mm size
Adenia obesum
Agave angustifolia
Euphorbia lactea
Euphorbia lactea cristate
Ficus petiolaris
Kalanchoe (most forms)
Pachypodium (most species)
Senecio mandraliscae

Larger growing species
Agave attenuata
Euphorbia trigona
Kalanchoe beharensis
Pachypodium geayi
Pachypodium lamerei
Yucca aloifolia
Yucca elephantipes

Recommended cactus

The following cactus are recommended for outdoor gardens.

50-300 mm height
Echinocereus cinerascens
Echinopsis species
Mammillaria compressa
Mammillaria geminispina
Mammillaria hahniana
Mammillaria pringlei
Mammillaria spinosissima
Notocactus leninghausii
Notocactus magnificus
Winterocereus aureispinus

300-900 mm height
Echinocactus grusonii
Espostoa species
Ferocactus species
Myrtillocactus cochal
Opuntia microdasys
Oreocereus trollii
Trichocereus grandiflora
Trichocereus huascha
Trichocereus spachianus

taller
Cereus peruvianus
Cleistocactus strausii
Opuntia ficus-indica
Oreocereus (most species)
Pachycereus marginatus
Trichocereus pachonoi
Trichocereus pasacana
Trichocereus peruvianus
Trichocereus scopulicolis
Trichocereus terscheckii

Flowering

Whereas all succulents can and do flower, not all are reliable or worthwhile in their flower show, colour or overall performance. The following is a list of recommended succulents.

Plant	Flower colour	Flowering season
Aeoniums (most species)	mostly bright yellow	spring
Aloes (most species)	orange/red	winter, spring, summer
Carpobrotus species	pink/yellow	variable
Cotyledon macrantha	bright orange	late winter
Cotyledon orbiculata	pale orange	late spring
Crassula ovata	pink and white	spring
Crassula falcata	bright pink/red	spring/autumn
Dorotheanthus bellidiformis *	mixed colours	winter/spring
Echeveria 'Black Prince'	red	autumn
Echeveria (most species)	orange/yellow	variable
Echeveria elegans	pink	spring
Echeveria pulidonis	bright yellow	spring
Euphorbia milii	red/yellow	any season
Euphorbias (most species)	yellow/green	spring
Faucaria species	yellow	autumn/winter
Graptopetalum bella (*Tacitus bellus*)	pink/red	early summer
Hesperaloe parviflora	red/pink	spring, summer, autumn
Kalanchoe blossfeldiana hybrids	mixed	variable
Kalanchoe 'Candy Cane'	pink	spring
Kalanchoe pumila	bright pink	spring
Kalanchoe tubiflora	red/orange	spring
Lampranthus	mixed	spring
Oscularia deltoides (mesemb)	pink	spring
Portulaca grandiflora *	mixed	summer
Sedum spectabile	pink	autumn
Sedum spectabile 'Autumn Joy'	burgundy	autumn
Yuccas (all species)	creamy white	summer

* These are annuals and can be very quick growing to fill up open spaces between bigger or slower growing plants. They are only grown for their masses of flowers, which last for several months.

Leaf colour changes

Many succulents undergo leaf colour changes through the seasons. Listed below are some of those that show the most reliable and dramatic changes. This may be significant to anyone who is designing a colour-coordinated garden.

Plant	Conditions	Colour changes
Aeonium 'Zwartkop'	summer	leaves turn from purple/brown to black
Crassula anomala	with any stress	leaves turn from green to bright red
Crassula ovata (all species)	stress	leaves turn from green to yellow and red
Echeveria (ruffled types)	autumn	leaf colours intensify and fringes colour up.
Echeveria 'Violet Queen'	frost and cold	leaves turn from bluish to pink
Sedum rubrotinctum	with any stress	leaves turn from green to red
Sempervivum (some species)	variable	leaves turn from green to burgundy

Succulents—some other uses

Bird attracting

All aloes and gasterias are well known for their ability to attract native birds to the garden.

Butterfly attracting

Sedum spectabile
Sedum spectabile 'Autumn Joy'
Lampranthus spp.

Edible

Carpobrotus (all species) From the Greek words karpo (fruit) and brota (edible things), with reference to their edible fruits.

Herbal and medicinal

Aloe vera, *Aloe vera* var. *chinensis* and *Aloe barbadensis* (all of these are forms of *Aloe vera*).
Aloe ferox
Aeonium lindleyi
Sempervivum tectorum
Yucca schidigera

Further research will be necessary to understand more about the medicinal uses of succulents. The internet is a good place to start a search for additional information.

Compatible non-succulent plants

There are many plants that will grow well with succulents and that will take the same conditions, but be very careful here. The balance of how they look together will be significant and they will either grow harmoniously or they will not. You will have to get this right from the start. This very highly recommended list of easily obtainable plants incorporates those with a proven track record.

Bedding plants
to 300 mm tall

Aechmea recurvata
(bromeliad)
Bromeliads
(hardy, dwarf)
Bulbs
(summer dormant)
California poppy
(*Eschscholzia californica*)
Carex
Chlorophytum comosum
"spider plant", good for
shade)
Festuca ovina var. *glauca*
Gazanias
Haemanthus coccineus
Lavenders
(dwarf forms)
Setcresia purpurea

Australian natives
Anigozanthos (dwarf)
(kangaroo paw)
Helichrysums

Shrubs
300-900 mm tall

Asclepias curassavica
Cycads
Echiums
Euphorbias
Helenium autumale
Kniphofias
Lavenders
Pennisetums
(decorative grasses)
Santolinas
"lavender cotton"
Senecio cineraria
"dusty miller"
Statice
Strelitzias

Australian natives
Anigozanthos species
"kangaroo paws"
Correa 'Dusky Bells'
Darwinia species
Leucophyta brownii
"cushion bush"
Xanthorrhoeas
"grass trees"

Specimen plants
1-2+ m tall

Chorisia speciosa
Cordyline australis
Echiums
Erythrinas
Livistona (fan palms)
Palms (select others)
Phoenix canariensis
(Canary Island palm)
Phormium tenax
Washingtonia robusta
"cotton palm"

Australian natives
Brachychitons
(some species)
Doryanthes excelsa
Doryanthes palmeri
Eucalyptus caesia
ssp. *magna* (2+ m)
Eucalyptus macrocarpa
Eucalyptus pressiana
Eucalyptus rhodantha

Echeverias

This table shows the single most popular group of succulents for the garden. There are dozens of species and hundreds of hybrids (indicated by '....') within the genus *Echeveria*. Below are some colourful and popular ones which may be available at your local garden centre.

Grow to 100 mm	Grow up to 200 mm	Larger growing
E. *bella*	E. *agavoides* 'Lipstick'	E. 'Afterglow'
E. *deffractens*	E. 'Black Prince'	E. 'Blue Curls'
E. *derenbergii*	E. 'Blue Surprise'	E. 'Blue Waves'
E. *elegans*	E. 'Curly Locks'	E. 'County Fair'
E. 'Emerald Ripple'	E. 'Doris Taylor'	E. 'Crinoline'
E. *globulosa*	E. *elegans*	E. *gibbiflora* 'Carunculata'
E. *linguifolia*	E. 'Lemon Twist'	E. *gigantea*
E. *minima*	E. *lindsayana*	E. 'Golden Glow'
E. 'Morning Beauty'	E. 'Lola'	E. 'Gypsy'
E. *nodulosa*	E. *macabeana*	E. 'Imbricata'
E. 'Perle von Nurnberg'	E. 'Morning Light'	E. 'Katella IV'
E. *pulvinata*	E. *pulidonis*	E. 'Mademoiselle'
E. *pulvinata* 'Frosty'	E. *peacockii*	E. 'Mauna Loa'
E. *purpusorum*	E. 'Red Edge'	E. 'Paul Bunyan'
E. *setosa* var. *diminuta*	E. 'Van Breen' cristata	E. 'Powder Blue'
E. *setosa*	E. *violescens*	E. 'Zorro'

Succulents as weeds

Any plant, when removed from its natural environment and introduced into a new one, has the potential to become weedy; that is, to grow and survive without care. Many exotic plants are able to invade the natural environment. The greatest danger from succulents is via trimmings which may re-root when improperly disposed of. Responsible management and after-care should be exercised when disposing of any plant waste to prevent it from establishing itself outside your garden. Never consider dumping garden clippings or waste of any kind in the bush!

If you live in the country or in suburban areas where there is still waste land or bush nearby and are planning landscapes using succulents, check with your local council to obtain a listing of plants which are prohibited or are not recommended for gardens in your area. If they do not have a list, ask to be transferred to the relevant state authority. Our gardens are for the plants of the world but the bush is only for our native species. Lets keep it that way!

Books and web sites

Recommended books

Anderson, M., 1999. *The Illustrated Encyclopedia of Cacti and Succulents*, Lorenz Books.
A useful book which describes many of the available cactus and succulents. While not garden centered, it does provide useful and detailed information on the care and maintenance of specific groups of plants. In hardbound and paperback editions, at about $80 and $35 respectively.

Cave, Y., 1996. *The Succulent Garden,* Florilegium.
Highly recommended, available through most better book shops at about $28.

Cave, Y., 2002. *Succulents for the Contemporary Garden*, Florilegium.
Available through most larger bookshops at about $40.

Huntington Gardens, 1995. *Dry Climate Gardening with Succulents*, Pantheon, New York.
Written for American conditions. Full of colourful ideas to try. Lists many available succulents as well as some rare and scarce ones. May need to be specially ordered. Around $60.

Morgan, D., 2004. *Succulents for the Mediterranean Garden*, Rosenberg.
Available through most larger bookshops for around $25.

Schulz, L., & Kapitany, A., 2006. *Echeveria Cultivars*, Schulz Publishing.
The only book of its kind. Hardbound, containing over 500 colour photographs. Also includes care, health and propagation. Available through all bookshops and from the authors. $49.95

Internet contacts

The Cactus and Succulent Plant Mall is an internet resource for all growers of cacti and succulent plants. It is regularly updated with information on cactus and succulent societies and suppliers of plants, seeds and literature on cacti and succulents. The Cactus and Succulent Plant Mall hosts webpages for more than 100 cactus and succulent organisations worldwide. Their list of societies provides useful first contacts for Australian and overseas societies. Visit them at: **http://www.cactus-mall.com**

The Cactus and Succulent Society of Australia Inc has a website which can provide contacts and links to other societies in Australia and overseas. Visit them at: **www.cssaustralia.org.au**

Index

Photo references in **bold**